Rock
Guitar Case
by Russ Shipton

Exclusive Distributors:
Music Sales Corporation
257 Park Avenue South, New York, NY 10010, USA
Music Sales Limited
8/9 Firth Street, London W1V 5TZ, England
Music Sales Pty. Limited
120 Rothschild Avenue, Rosebery, NSW2018, Australia

Introduction

The Rock and Roll Guitar Case Chord Book is a reference book produced specifically for the rock guitarist. Designed for easy and quick access to the most used chord forms, it is also tailored to fit into your instrument case.

The first section shows those chord positions most used by professionals, grouped together by key. The common chord triads of tonic, sub-dominant and dominant chords are shown on one page, with four positions for each. The most compatible positions can quickly be chosen for a particular arrangement.

The relative minor triad follows the major triad on the facing page – so no turning over is necessary when an arrangement involves both major and minor chords.

In case you are not familiar with the chord window diagrams used in this book, here is an explanation:

Chord Windows

The G Major Chord

 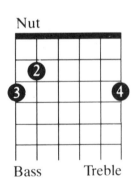

● = Left Hand Finger Indications

Those strings with no finger indications on them can be played open, unless an 'x' is marked beneath the string – then the string must be damped, or not struck.

One common feature of rock chords is the 'barré' or 'bar':

The A♭ * Major Chord

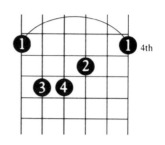

4th

The barré or bar:
The first finger goes across all the strings at the 4th fret.

The curved line between the '1' finger indications means that the first finger must go across *all* the strings between, as well as the first and the sixth strings. Not all the strings need be pressed down hard – in this case the third, fourth and fifth strings are covered by other fingers on higher frets, so only the first, second and sixth strings have to be firmly pressed.

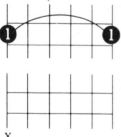

This means that every string is pressed down by the 1st finger at the same fret

' x ' under a string means that the string is not played or should be damped

X

---

* *The usual name is given to those chords that can have two, i.e. the A♭ here may sometimes be called a G♯ chord. This is known as the 'enharmonic' equivalent.*

Notes on Playing Rock and Roll

Bar Chords
Rock guitarists use many bar chords and partial chord forms. Knowing a variety of these is essential to producing the right sounds. Generally capos are not used in rock music, so a knowledge of the shapes and chord forms in all the different keys is imperative.

Damping
The 'open' sound involved with more traditional music is largely discarded in rock. So bar chords and damping are used for a much tighter sound. Damping with the left hand is particularly important. The left hand fingers release their pressure on the strings after they have been struck by the right hand. But they maintain contact and so stop the sound soon after the strings ring. The strong rock rhythms that we hear today would be impossible without left hand damping.

Root Notes
'Straight' chords are normally used in rock music. If more notes are added to the chords, a jazzy flavour creeps in. Though some inversions are shown in this book, most chord forms have the root of the chord as the bass note. These provide a solid basis for rock and roll.

Alternative Fingering
Some chords can be fingered in different ways. Two important alternatives in rock and roll playing are the use of the left hand thumb on the sixth string, and the third finger bar when using an **A shape**. For example, when fingering the **B♭** chord with a first finger bar on the first fret, the third finger can bar the second, third and fourth strings at the third fret. This releases the other two fingers, and can allow more speed and attack.

Major & Minor Chord Triads

Chord Positions

Chords can be played in many different positions on the fretboard. You are sure to be familiar with those positions near the nut end of the neck, in the commonly used guitar keys. Here is the chord window for the **E** chord, followed by a photo of the left hand position:

The E (Major) Chord ('open' position)

 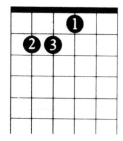

The same notes that make up the **E** chord can be played further up the fretboard:

The E (Major) Chord (bar 4th position)

 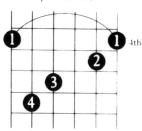

Though the notes may not be in the same order as before, or may not be duplicated in a similar way, the same three notes are played. It is every bit as much an **E** chord as the 'open' position chord.

Similarly, instead of the usual lower 'open' position for the **C** chord, these are two other possibilities:

The C (Major) Chord (bar 3rd & bar 8th positions)

 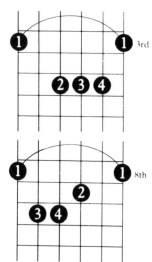

Chord Fingering

Sometimes a 'full' 6-string version of a chord is not required, or is not as flexible as a smaller version. As an example, let us take the second **E** chord position shown on the previous page. Here are four different fingering possibilities:

The E (Major) Chord (bar 4th position)

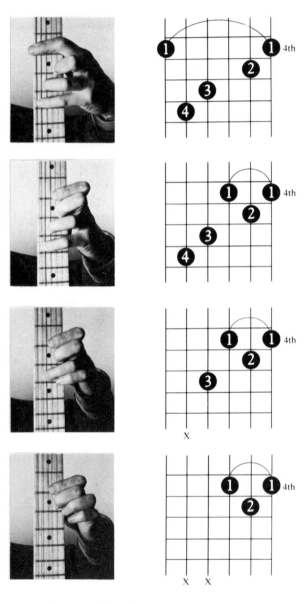

x = string not played

In the third example, the 5th string should not be played. In the last example, both the 4th and 5th strings should not be played. The open 6th string can be struck if required.

There are great advantages of mobility in using the smaller fingerings – slides, hammer-ons and pull-offs, as well as chord changes in general, are more easily performed.

In a similar way to the **E** chord shown on the previous page, the **C** chord, bar 8th position can be fingered in these ways:

The C (Major) Chord (bar 8th position)

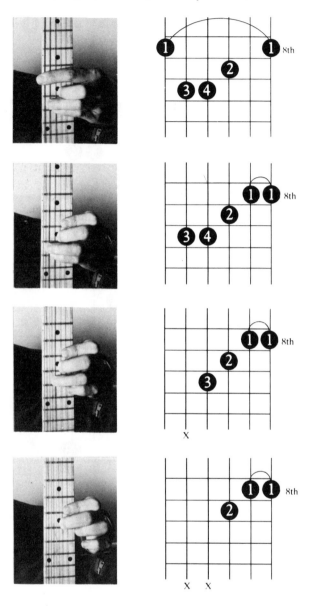

The last two examples would be useful for slides, and free one or two fingers for the hammer-ons and pull-offs.

Some of the various fingering possibilities shown above are included in the first section of the book. They are also very relevant to the moveable chord shapes discussed in section two.

The choice of a particular fingering and position will depend on the other chords in the sequence – how they are fingered, and in what position – and the type of sound required. Your musical taste will be allowed more freedom of expression the more variations you know.

Key of C Major

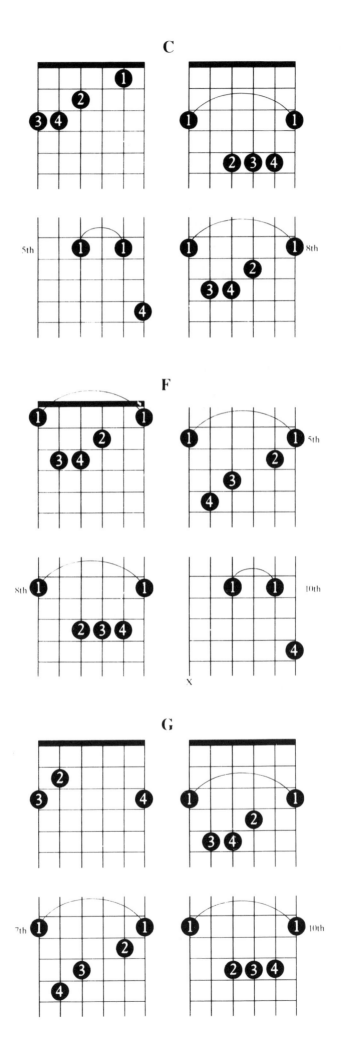

8

Relative Key of A Minor

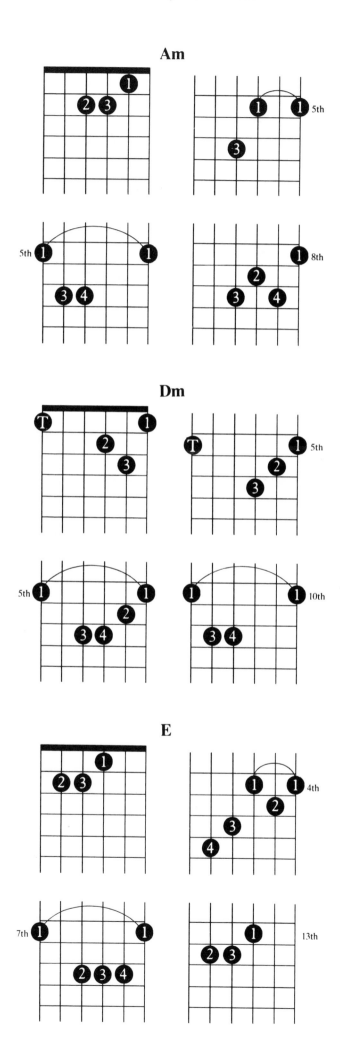

Key of D♭ * Major

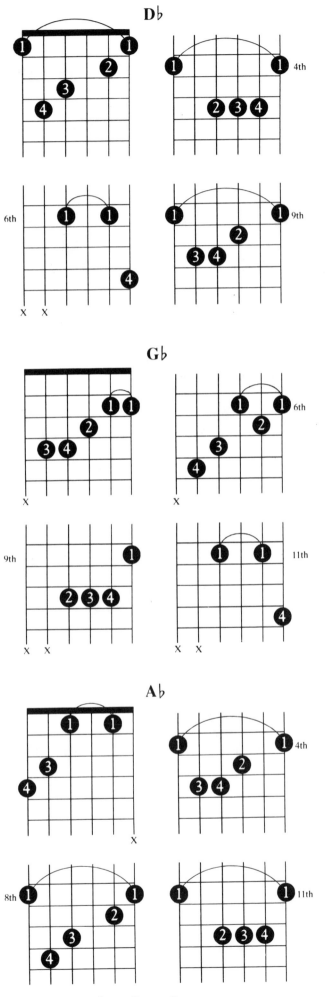

* See note at foot of page 3

Relative Key of B♭ * Minor

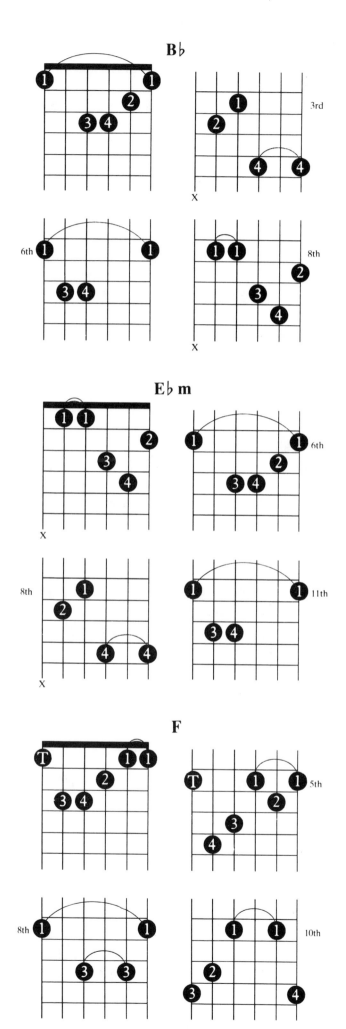

See note at foot of page 3

Key of D Major

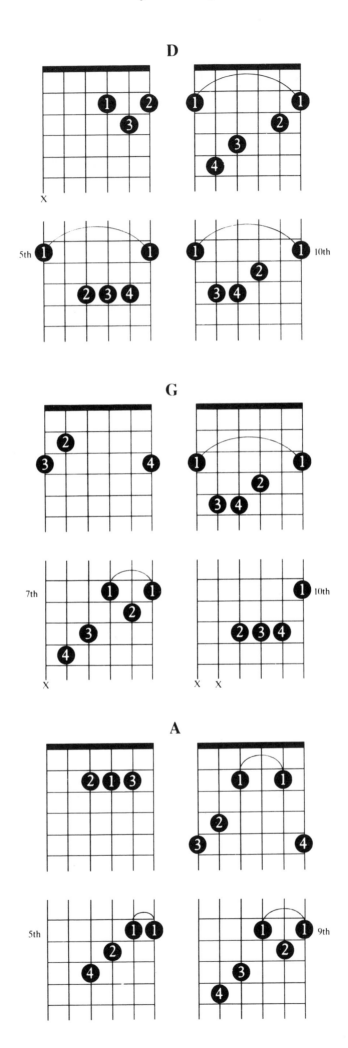

Relative Key of B Minor

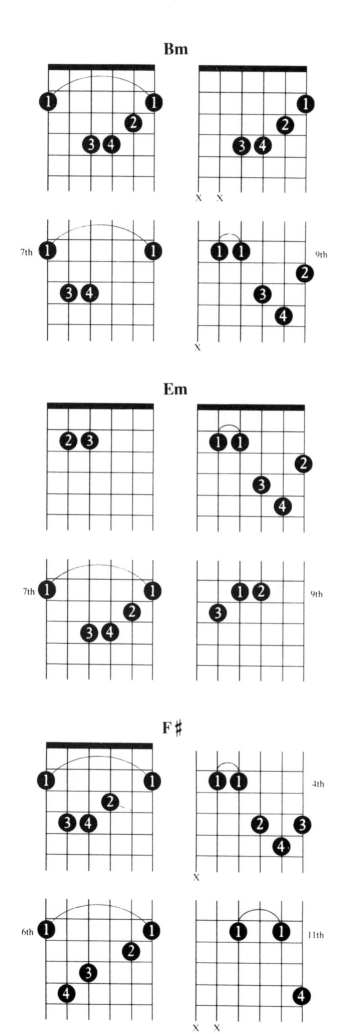

Key of E♭ * Major

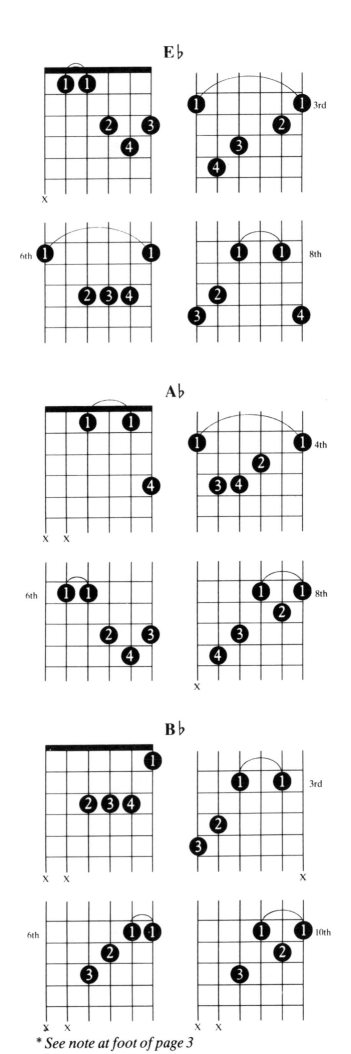

* See note at foot of page 3

Relative Key of C Minor

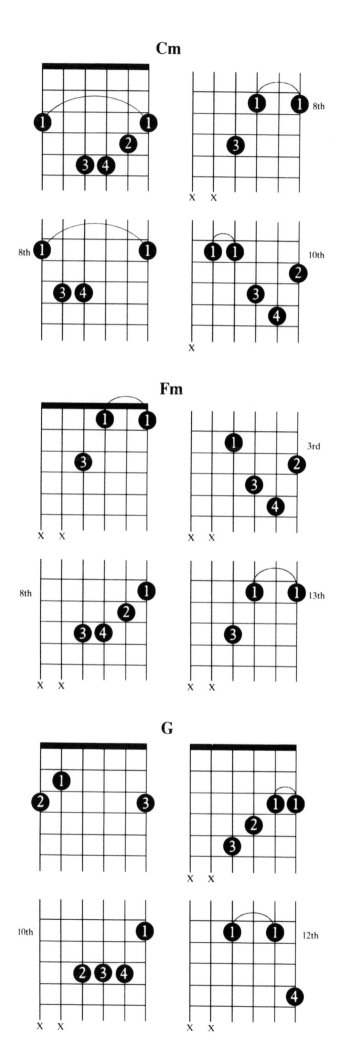

Key of E Major

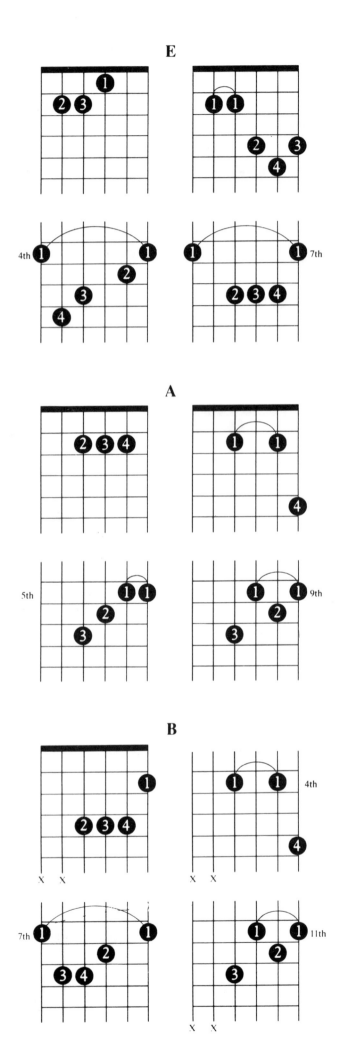

Relative Key of C♯ * Minor

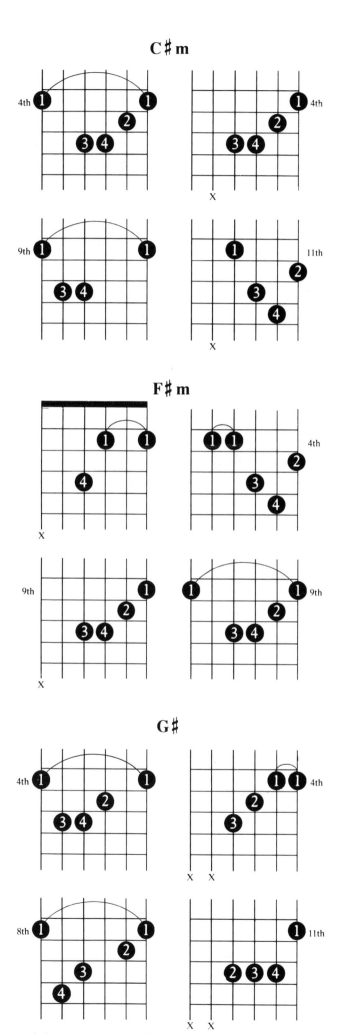

C♯m

F♯m

G♯

See note at foot of page 3

Key of F Major

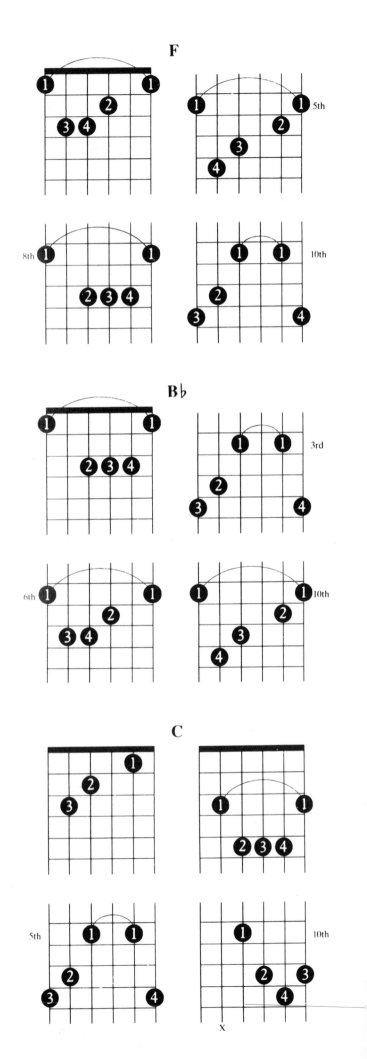

Relative Key of D Minor

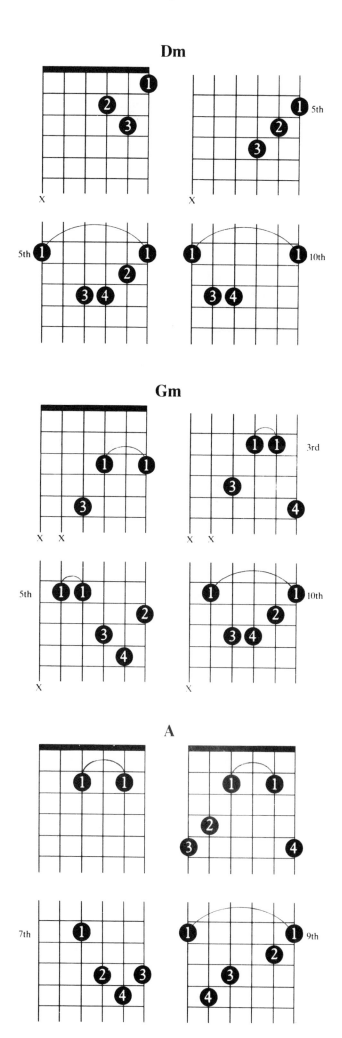

Key of G♭ * Major

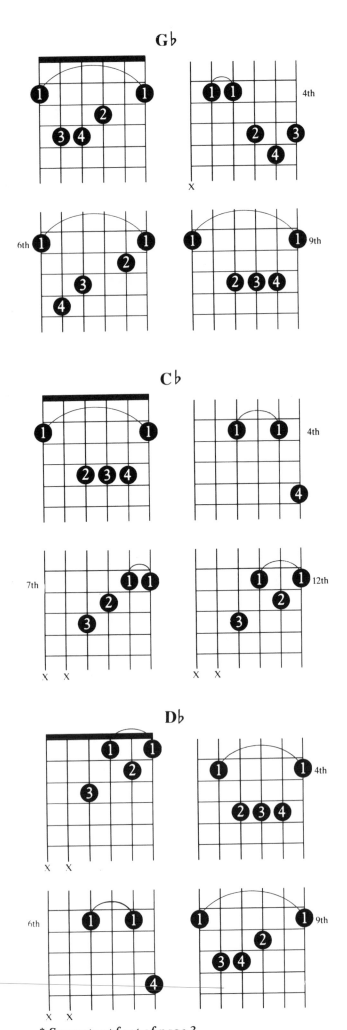

G♭

C♭

D♭

See note at foot of page 3

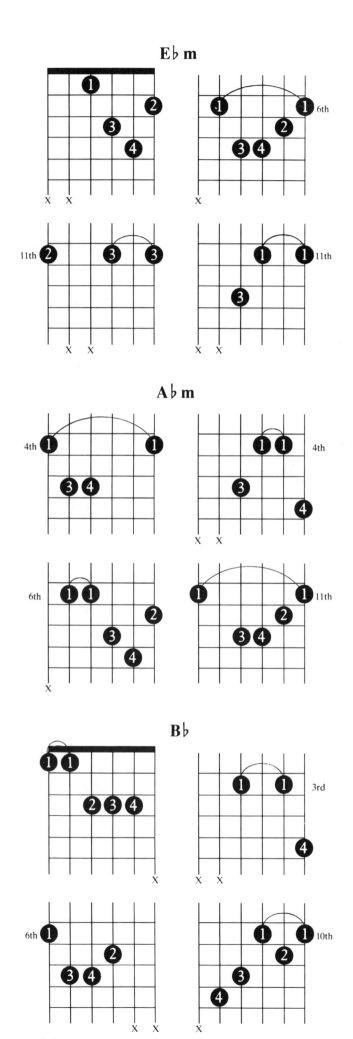

Key of G Major

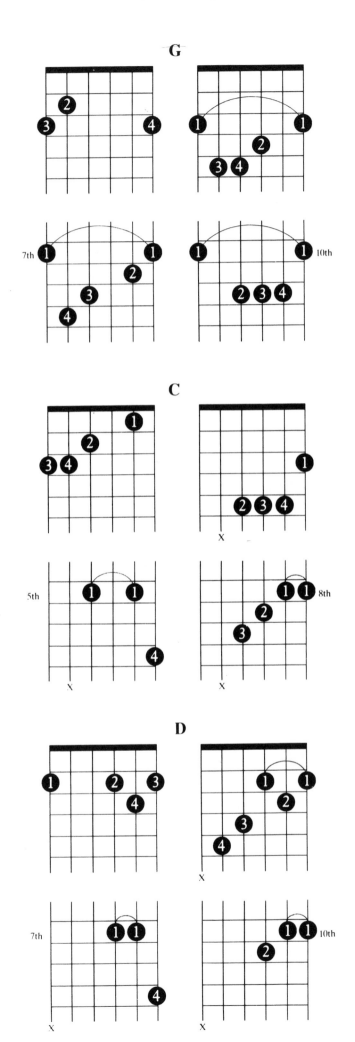

Relative Key of E Minor

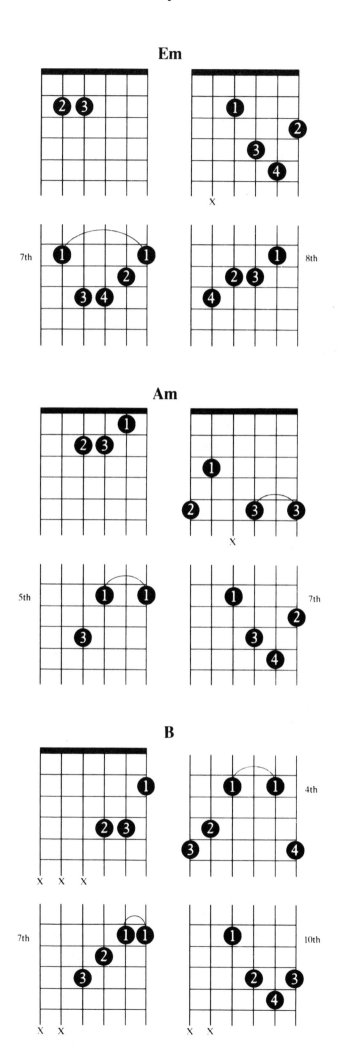

Key of A♭ * Major

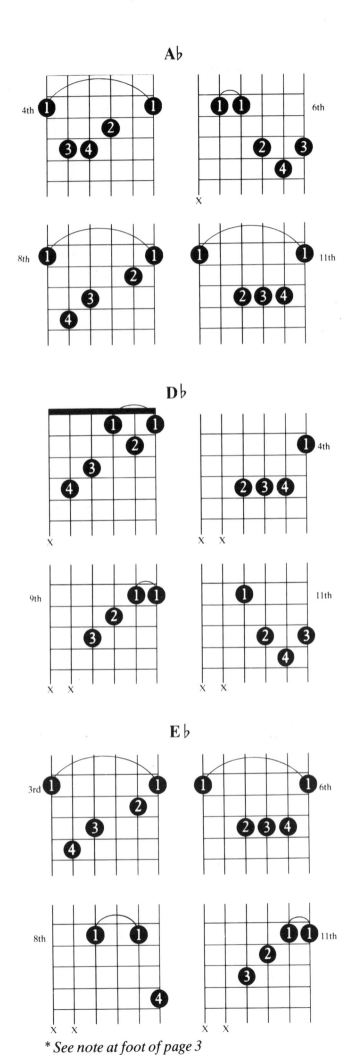

Relative Key of F Minor

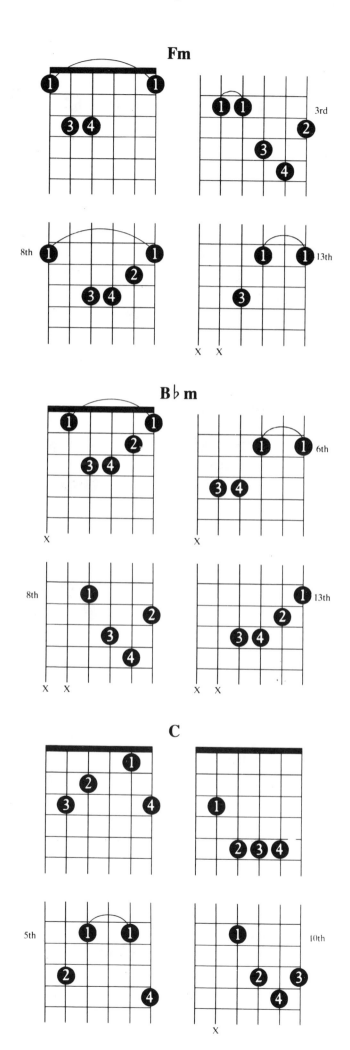

Key of A Major

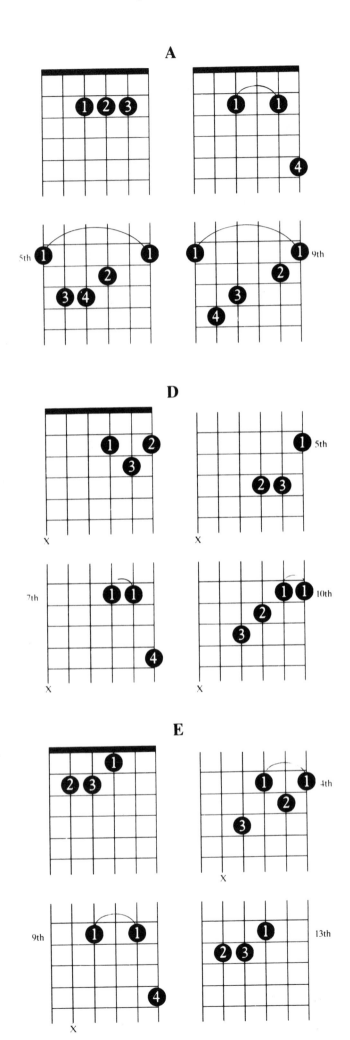

Relative Key of F♯ *Minor

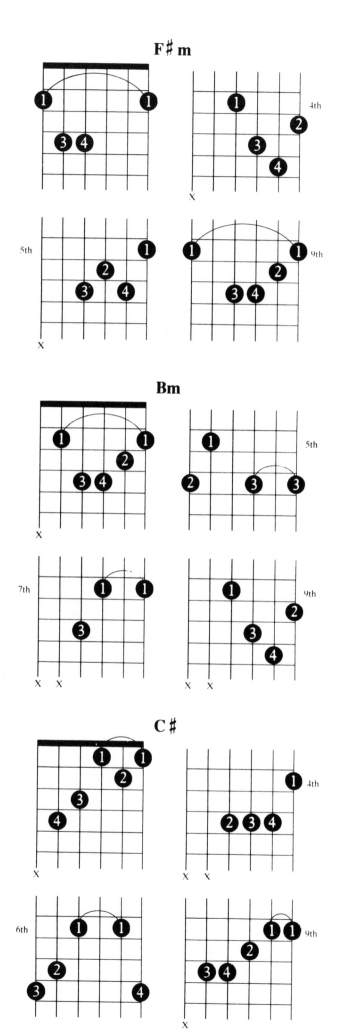

* See note at foot of page 3

Key of B♭ * Major

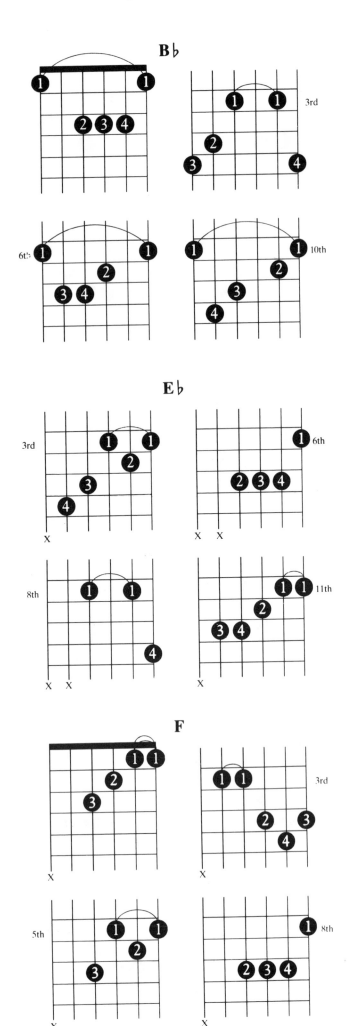

* See note at foot of page 3

Relative Key of G Minor

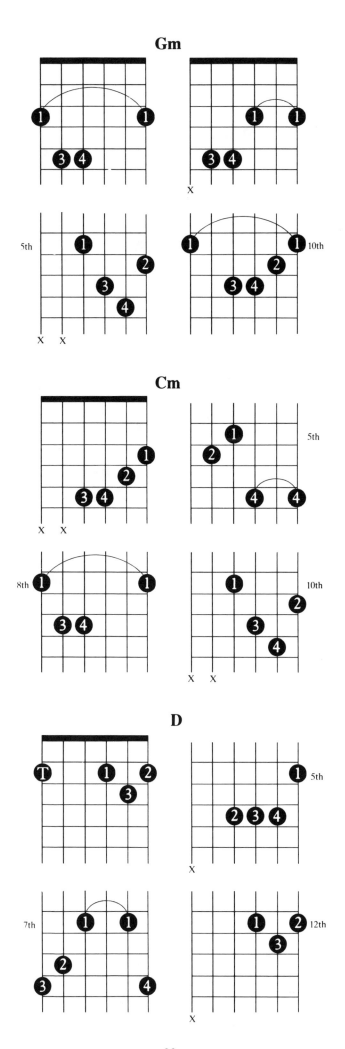

Key of B Major

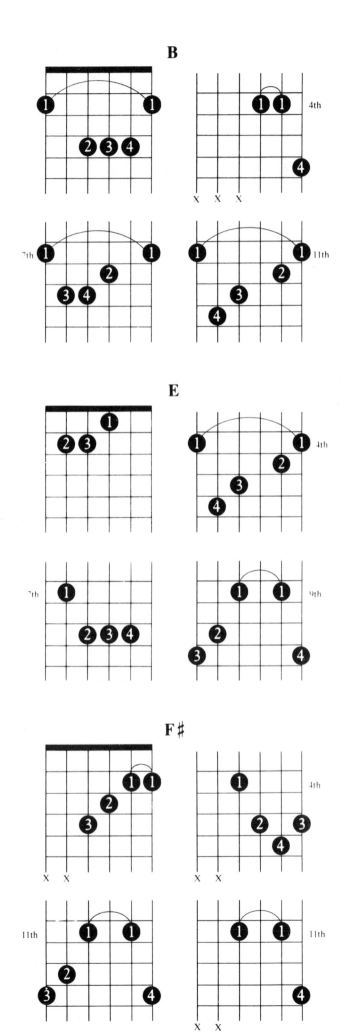

30

Relative Key of G♯ * Minor

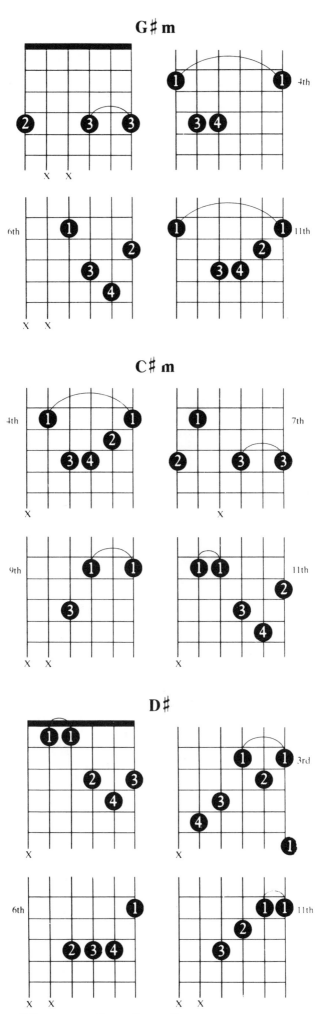

G♯ m

C♯ m

D♯

See note at foot of page 3

Moveable Chord Shapes

Music involves patterns. In scales, chords and melodies, there are patterns that repeat themselves. Don't attempt to learn music theory just parrot fashion, and you will soon appreciate the simplicity of how music is represented.

Just as notes repeat themselves: **a, a♯/b♭, b, c, c♯/d♭, d, d♯/e♭, e, f, f♯/g♭, a, a♯/b♭, b**, etc., so do chords. On the guitar, the open strings (from the 6th) are: **e, a, d, g, b, e**. The most-used chords (particularly in rock) have the root note (which gives the chord its name) on one of the three bass strings. Therefore, if you know the note sequence above, it's easy to name the same chord shape as it moves up the fretboard. Let's have a look at the **E** chord:-

The E (Major) Chord

 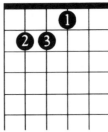

Root note (on 6th String) =**e**

The F (Major) Chord

 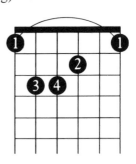

Root note =**f**

The F♯/G♭ (Major) Chord

 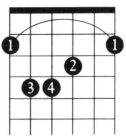

Root note =**f♯/g♭**

So long as *all* the strings change upwards or downwards by the same number of frets (or semitones), the quality of the chord will remain the same – only the pitch changes. In other words, the E shape above is an **E Major** Chord, and the same shape used further up the fretboard with a barre will remain a Major Chord, because all the notes go up by the same amount.

Here's another example:

The A (Major) Chord

 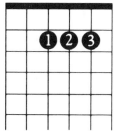

Root note (on 5th String)=**a**

The A♯/B♭ (Major) Chord

Root note=**a♯/b♭**

The B (Major) Chord

 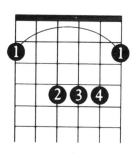

Root note=**b**

So the root note is on the fifth string in this case, and the A chord becomes a **B♭** when barring the first fret, a **B** when barring the second fret, and a **C** when barring the third fret. Carry on up the fretboard with that shape, naming the chords as you go.

Remember that the quality of the chord remains the same as you move the same shape up the fretboard. Therefore if you move a minor chord up, it remains a minor chord – only the pitch changes.

Sometimes there are two or more common ways of fingering a particular chord in the same place on the fretboard. Then you have a choice of which shape you can use as a moveable one. The **E (dominant)** seventh chord, for example, is often fingered in two ways – with or without the little finger.

Most shapes, with or without barre, can be used further up the fretboard, but often certain strings should be damped (with the left hand normally) or left alone. Occasionally open strings will fit with the notes that are fretted – then they can be hit if required.

Root 6 Chords (Major & Dominant)

Basic Shape

Moveable Shape

E

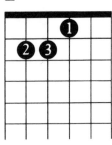

F

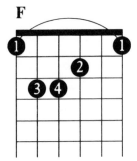

E = root

E maj 7

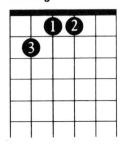

F maj 7

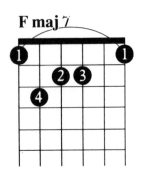

E7

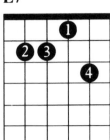

F7

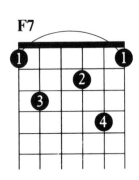

E9

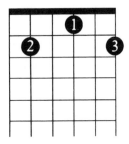

F9

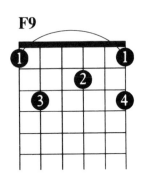

Root 6 Chords (Major & Dominant)

Basic Shape   **Moveable Shape**

E aug 9

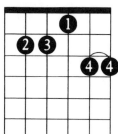

F aug 9

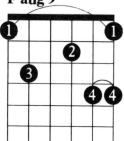

E6

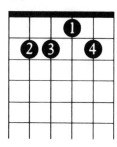

F6

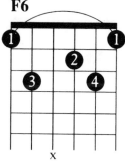

Esus

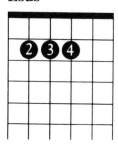

Fsus

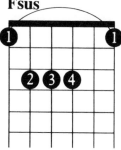

E° (diminished)

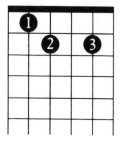

F°

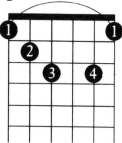

Root 6 Chords (Major & Dominant)

Basic Shape

Moveable Shape

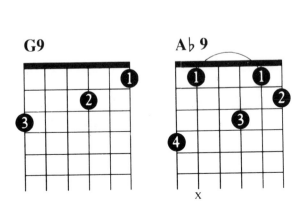

G

A♭

G7

A♭ 7

G6

A♭ 6

G9

A♭ 9

Root 6 Chords (Minor)

Basic Shape   **Moveable Shape**

Em
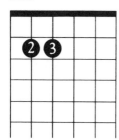

Fm
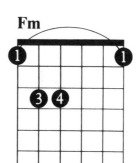

Em7
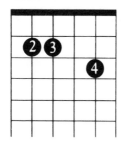

Fm7
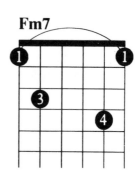

Em6
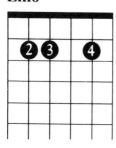

Fm6
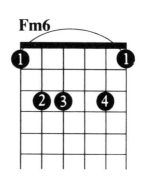

Em9
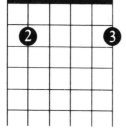

Fm9
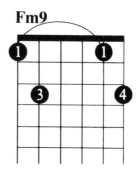

Root 5 Chords (Major & Dominant)

Basic Shape

Moveable Shape

A

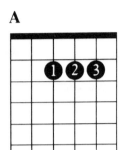

B♭

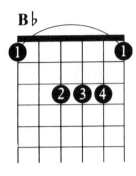

A maj 7

B♭ maj 7

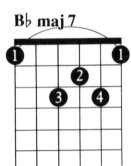

A7

B♭ 7

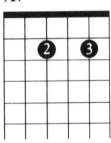

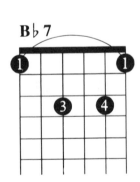

A9

B♭ 9

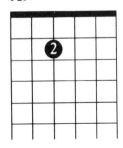

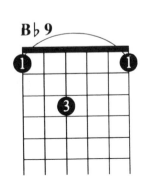

Root 5 Chords (Major & Dominant)

Basic Shape

Moveable Shape

A11

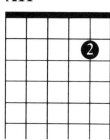

B♭ 11

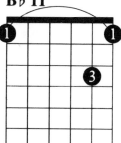

A6

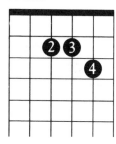

B♭ 6

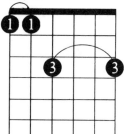

A sus

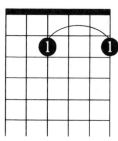

B♭ sus

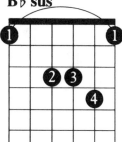

A-5 (flattened 5th)

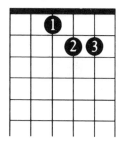

B♭ -5

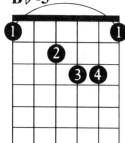

Root 5 Chords (Major & Dominant)

Basic Shape   **Moveable Shape**

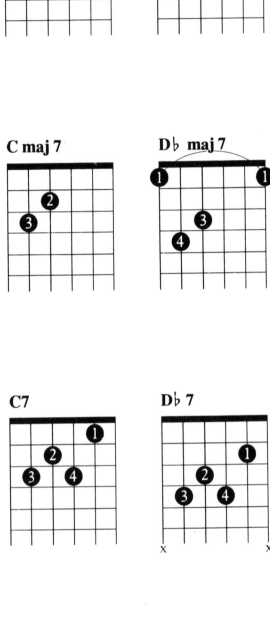

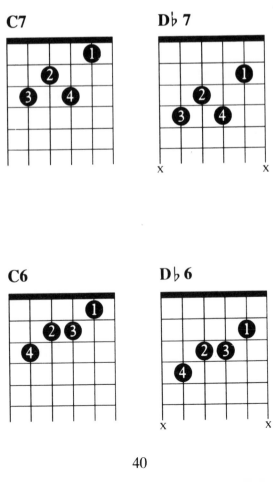

40

Root 5 Chords (Minor)

Basic Shape

Moveable Shape

Am
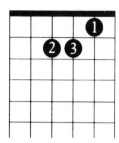

B♭m
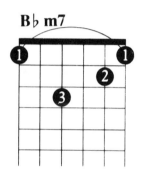

Am7
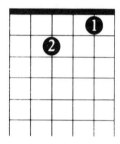

B♭m7

Am6
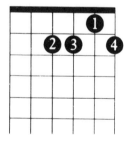

B♭m6

Bm9
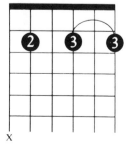

Cm9
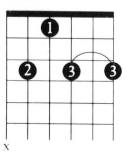
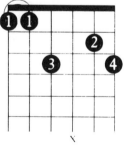

Root 4 Chords (Major & Dominant)

Basic Shape   ## Moveable Shape

D 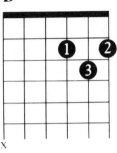   **E♭**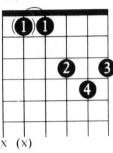

D maj 7 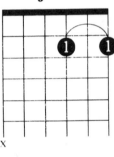   **E♭ maj 7**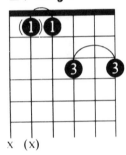

D7 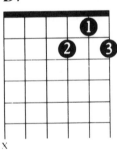   **E♭ 7**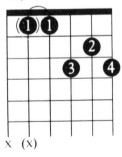

D6 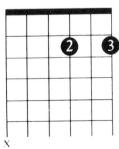   **E♭ 6**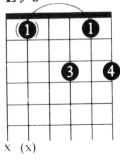

Root 4 Chords (Major & Dominant)

Basic Shape   ## Moveable Shape

D9

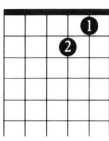

E♭ 9

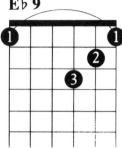

D°

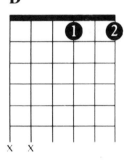

E♭ °

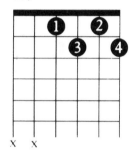

E+ (augmented)

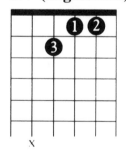

F+

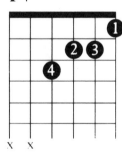

F maj 7

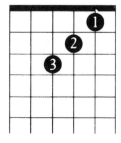

G♭ maj 7

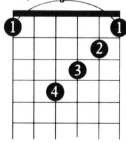

Root 4 Chords (Minor & 'Sus')

Basic Shape

Moveable Shape

Dm
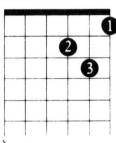

E♭ m
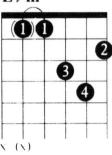

Dm7
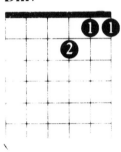

E♭ m7
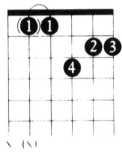

Dm6
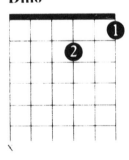

E♭ m6
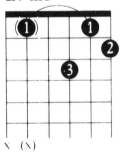

D sus
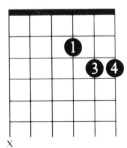

E♭ sus
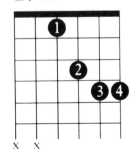

Rock Chord Sequences

In section 1 you looked at the main chords in every major and minor key. In section 2 you greatly expanded your knowledge of chords by learning the most useful moveable chord shapes. To help you on your way to becoming a tasteful and interesting player, here finally are some chord sequences that employ many of the ideas that you have examined so far.

Before trying the sequences on the following pages, here are some useful notes on using different fingerings and positions in the various keys:-

When you want to produce a very strong rhythm, it is usually better to use bar chords.

Normally it is better to use positions of chords that are in roughly the same area of the guitar, or to move gradually from one area of the guitar to another. There is usually a suitable chord fingering and position to be found – you just have to look for it!

Experiment with half-bars, not only with the first finger, but also with the second or third fingers. These greatly aid mobility and smooth playing. It does depend, though, on how flexible your finger joints are.

Experiment with damping – the left hand can do most of the work most of the time, but the right hand heel can drop down to the bass strings for a heavier damp sometimes. If a complete damp is required, the flat of the right hand can be used to muffle all the strings.

Successful arrangements of songs often involve one set of chord positions for accompanying the verse and/or chorus, and another set for a musical break – the second set of chords are usually higher up the fretboard. Sometimes the melody, or part of it, can be picked out from the chord shapes. Often you need to try different keys or different sets of shapes to get the best sound for the particular piece. It's always worth experimenting!

Rock Sequences

This sequence involves the **E** & **A** shapes. When you are familiar with it in the key of **G**, try doing the same sequence in **G♯**, or **A♭**.

Try using your left hand 3rd finger barred across the 2nd, 3rd and 4th strings.

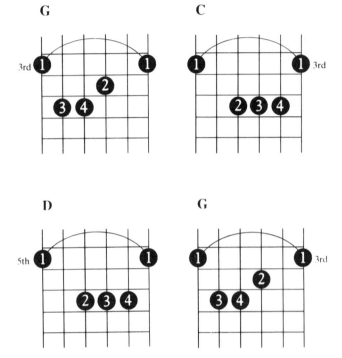

Using one version of the **E7** shape, try this sequence in the key of **F**.

Now use the version with the little finger added on the 2nd string.

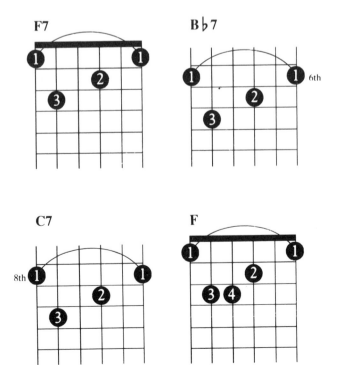

Rock Sequences

Here's a minor chord sequence with all positions on the 5th fret.

As with all these sequences, do the same thing in different positions on the fretboard, noting what key you're in and what chords you're playing each time.

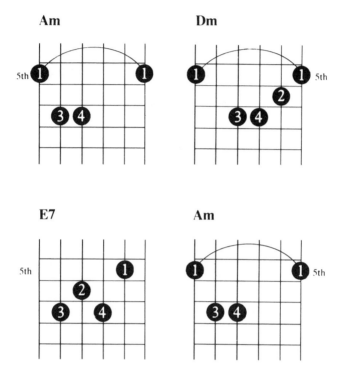

E♭ is quite a common key for keyboards – and not too difficult for the guitarist once he gets used to it. Here I've shown a very common sequence involving major and minor chords.

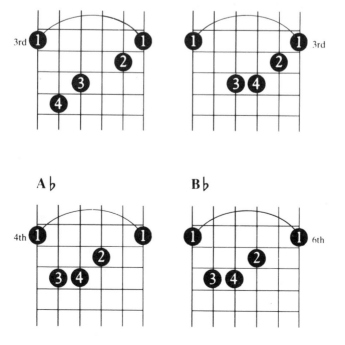

Rock Sequences

This key is a favourite guitar key but the sequence uses bars. The 3rd finger slides up to each new position, and thus can be used as an anchor.

This is an example where non-root notes are used on the bass.

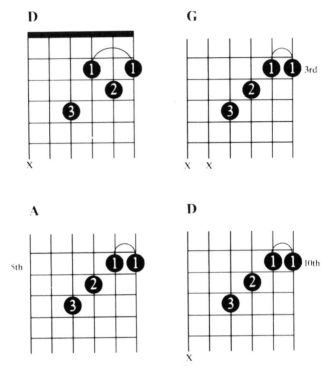

Here is another sequence which allows changes to be quick and smooth – the 2nd & 3rd fingers go down in front of the bar, and then the same shape moves along the fretboard.

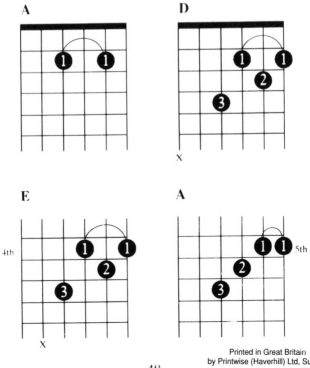

Printed in Great Britain
by Printwise (Haverhill) Ltd, Suffolk.

2/97 (27173)